Desert Friends:
An Arizona Animal Adventure

By Stephanie Wiggins

Dedication

To Jon Anthony,

A nature lover with a heart as wide as the Arizona skies, and a curiosity as boundless as its landscapes. This book is a window into the wild world of animals that call Arizona home, from the mighty mountain lions to the tiny horned toads. May their stories fill you with wonder and inspire a lifelong journey of discovery and respect for our fellow earth inhabitants. Here's to the adventures that await and the tales of nature that will forever bind us.

With all my love and a trail of paw prints,
Auntie Steph

Copyright © 2024 by Stephanie Wiggins
All rights reserved. No part of this publication may be reproduced, distributed, or transmitted in any form or by any means, including photocopying, recording, or other electronic or mechanical methods, without the prior written permission of the publisher, except in the case of brief quotations embodied in critical reviews and certain other noncommercial uses permitted by copyright law.

Gila Monster

Gila monsters are fascinating creatures that live in the deserts of the southwestern United States and northern Mexico. They are one of only two types of venomous lizards in the world, but don't worry, they are very shy and prefer to avoid people. Gila monsters have thick, bumpy skin with beautiful patterns that can be black, pink, orange, or yellow, making them look like they're wearing a colorful, beaded coat. They are quite slow-moving and spend most of their time hiding under the ground, coming out mainly to eat or sunbathe. Their favorite foods are eggs, small birds, and mice. Despite their fierce name and venomous bite, Gila monsters are pretty cool animals who play their own special role in the desert's ecosystem.

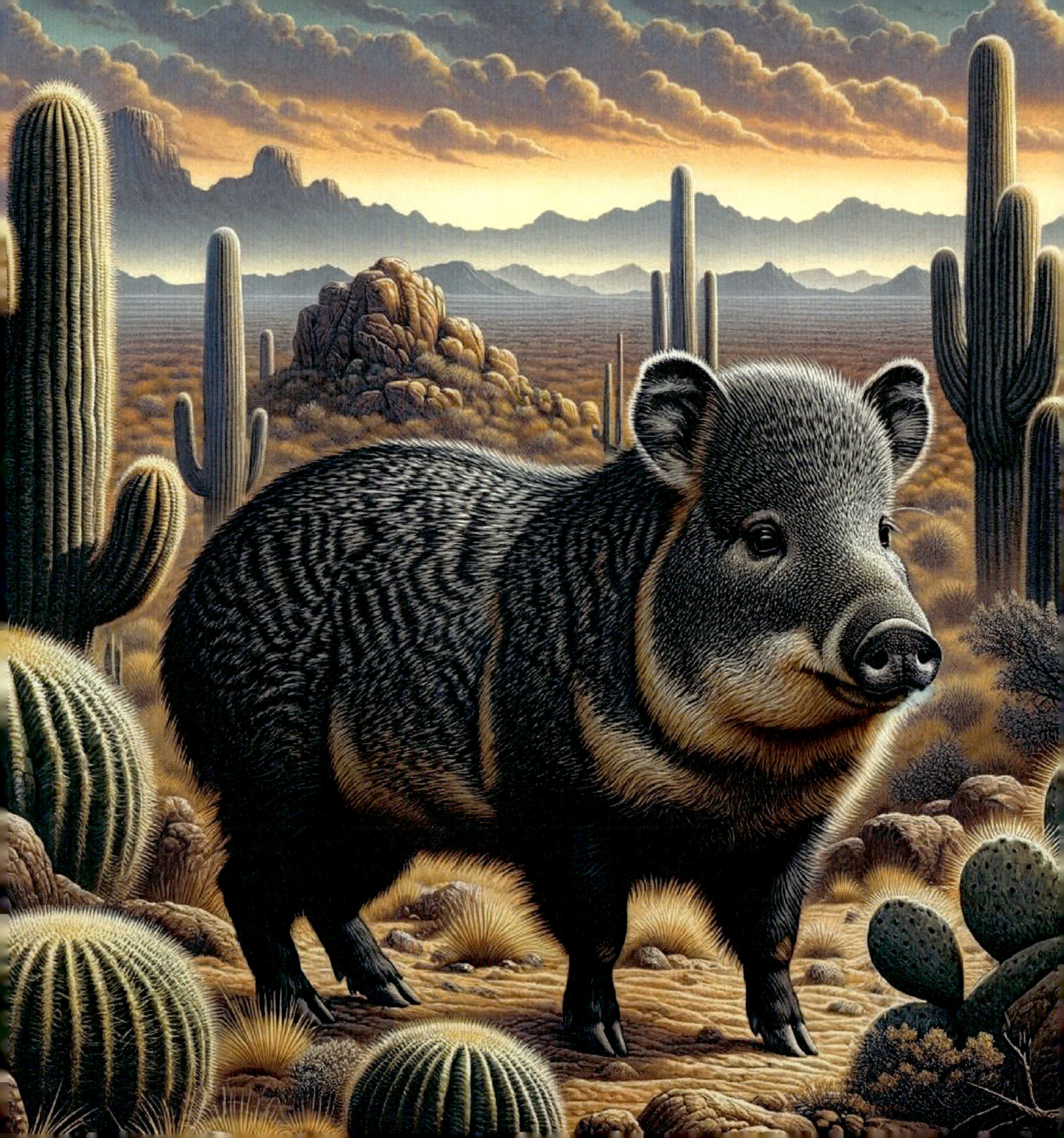

Javelina

Javelinas, also known as peccaries, are interesting little animals that might look a bit like pigs, but they're actually quite different! They live in the deserts and forests of North and South America, and they love to stick together in groups called herds. Javelinas have short, coarse hair, and some have a dark collar of fur around their necks, which looks like they're wearing a little coat. Despite their tough appearance, javelinas are herbivores, which means they mostly eat plants, like cacti, fruits, and roots. They have a strong sense of smell to help them find food and recognize each other, but their eyesight isn't very good. Javelinas are pretty shy around people and would rather run away than cause any trouble. They're really interesting creatures that show us how diverse and wonderful nature can be!

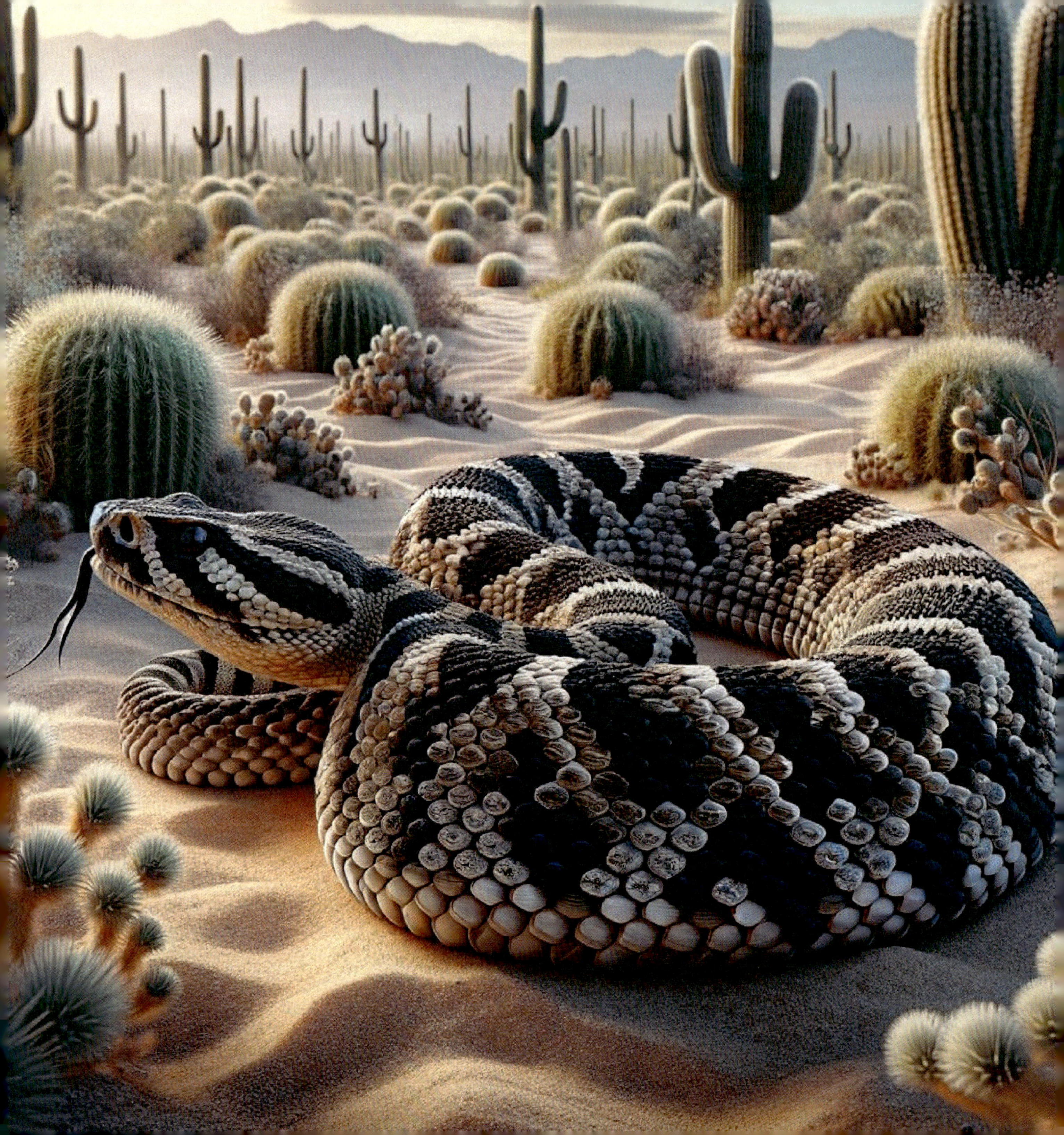

Diamondback Rattlesnake

The diamondback rattlesnake is an amazing creature that you might find slithering in the deserts and forests of the southwestern United States. They're known for the unique rattle sound they make with their tails, which they use to warn others to stay away. This rattlesnake has a pattern of diamond-shaped markings on its back, which is how it got its name. It can grow to be quite long, up to seven feet, but most are about four feet long. Diamondback rattlesnakes are important to the environment because they help control the populations of small animals and rodents. They use their sharp fangs to inject venom into their prey, which helps them catch their food. Even though they might sound a bit scary, they usually only bite if they feel threatened. It's always best to admire them from a safe distance and never try to touch or disturb them.

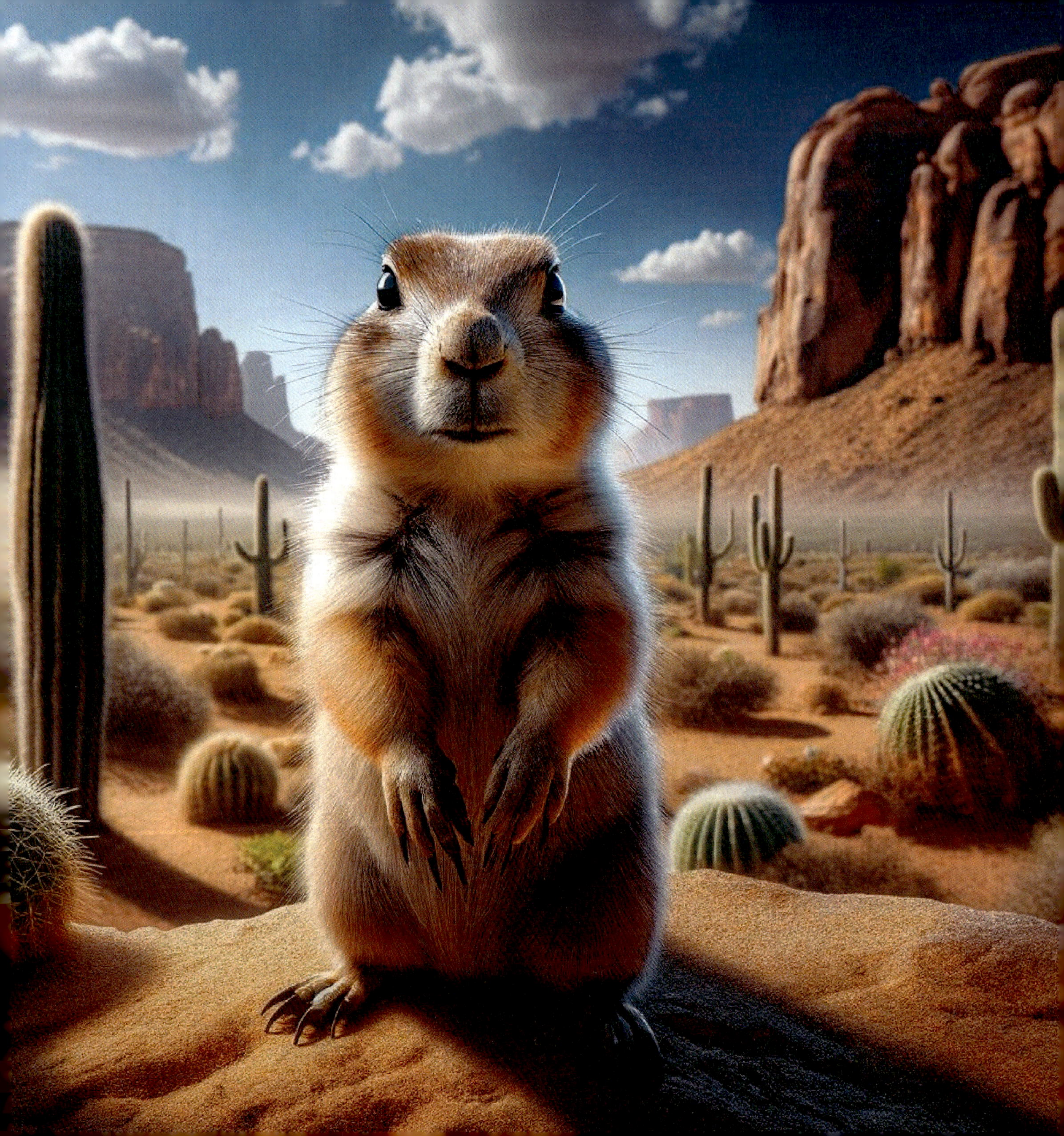

Prairie Dog

Prairie dogs are adorable, small animals that live in the grasslands and deserts of North America. They are not actually dogs, but a type of rodent, and they get their name because their calls sound a bit like a dog's bark. Prairie dogs are very social creatures and live together in large groups called towns, which can spread over many acres of land. Their homes are underground burrows, which have different rooms for sleeping, storage, and even nurseries for their babies. Prairie dogs are great at standing on their hind legs to look out for danger and use a special language of barks to talk to each other, warning their friends if a predator is near. They mostly eat plants, like grasses and herbs, making them important for keeping the ecosystem healthy. Watching a prairie dog town can be really fun, as they play, groom each other, and work together to take care of their families.

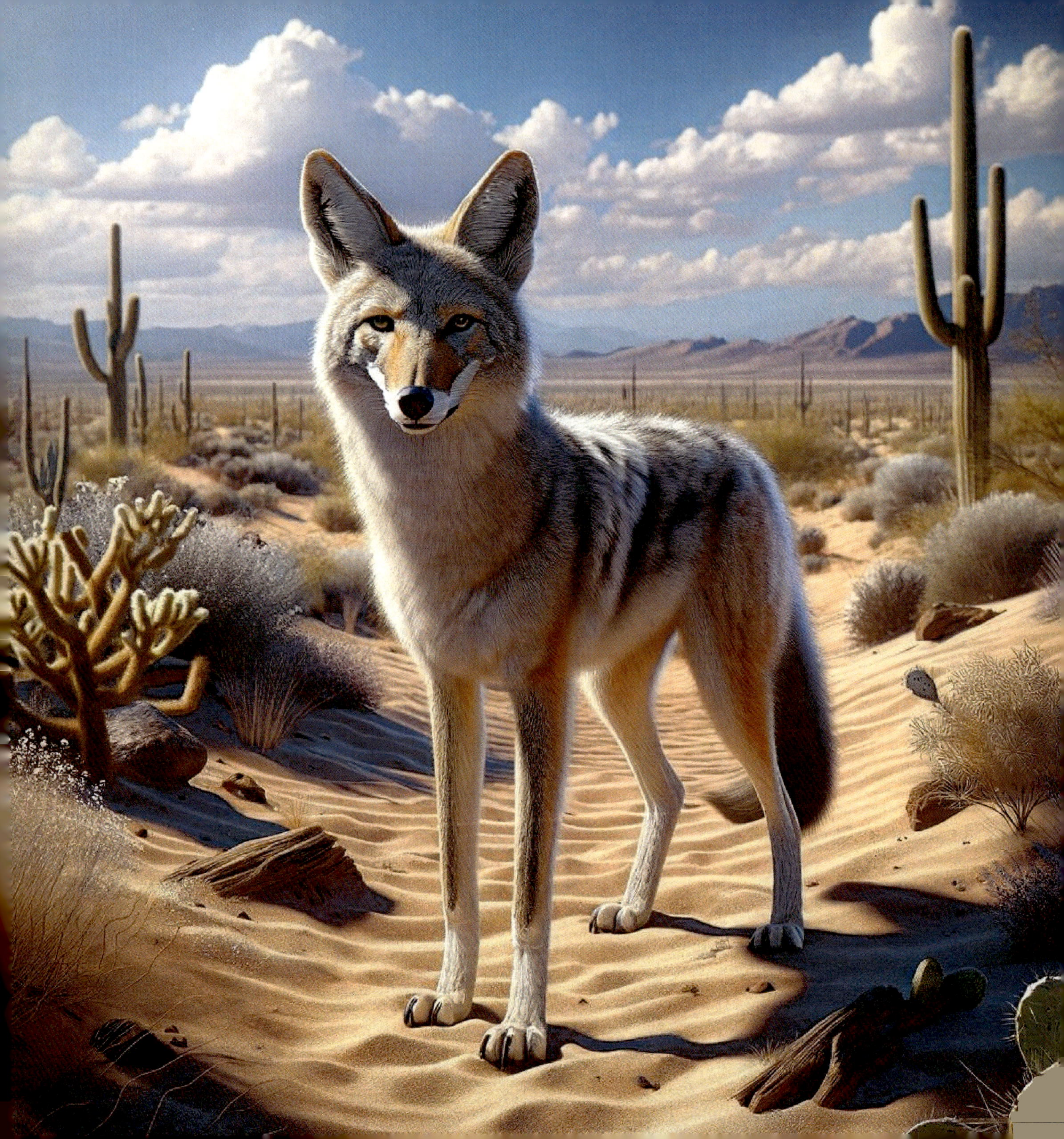

Coyote

Coyotes are wild animals that look a bit like the dogs we have as pets, but they live outdoors and can take care of themselves. They have a slim body, a bushy tail, and their fur can be gray, white, or brown, which helps them blend into their surroundings. Coyotes are very smart and adaptable, meaning they can live in many different places like forests, deserts, and even close to cities. They are mostly active at night, which is called being nocturnal, and they have an amazing sense of hearing and smell to help them find food. Coyotes eat almost anything, including fruits, insects, and small animals. They are known for their beautiful howling sound, which they use to talk to each other across long distances. Even though they are wild, coyotes play an important role in nature by helping control the number of rodents and other small animals. It's cool to learn about coyotes, but remember, if you ever see one, it's best to admire them from afar and not try to get close.

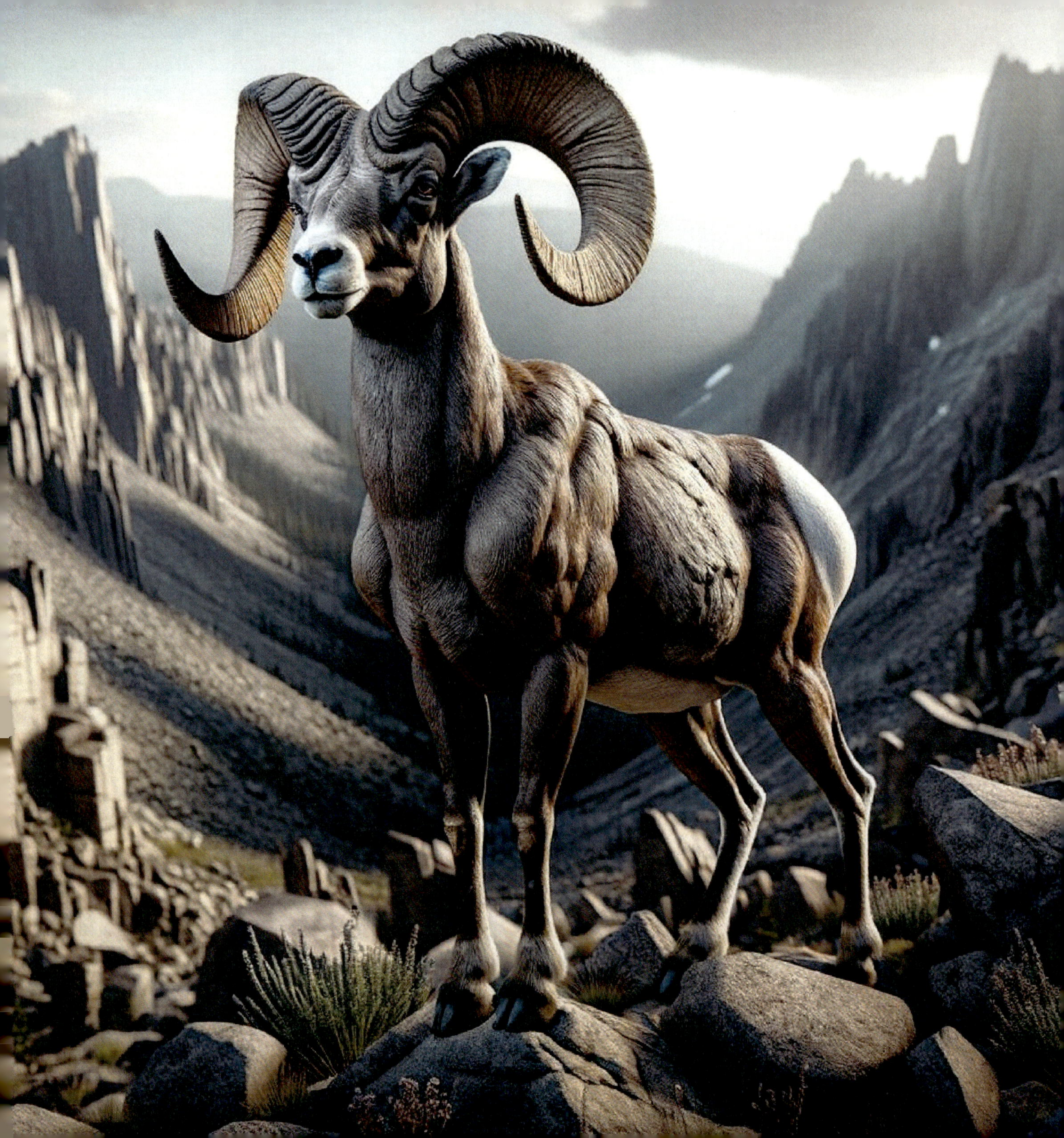

Bighorn Sheep

Big horned sheep in Arizona are amazing animals that love to climb and jump on the steep, rocky mountains. They have strong, muscular legs and hooves that grip onto the rocks, making them excellent climbers. Their most famous feature is their large, curved horns that look like big loops. These horns can be used to protect themselves and to show off during friendly battles with other sheep. Their fur is a light brown color, which helps them stay camouflaged, or hidden, in their natural desert and mountain homes. Big horned sheep are herbivores, which means they eat plants, like grass and leaves. They are very social animals and often stick together in groups to help look out for predators. Watching these incredible creatures expertly move up and down the mountains is a real treat, and they are an important part of Arizona's wildlife.

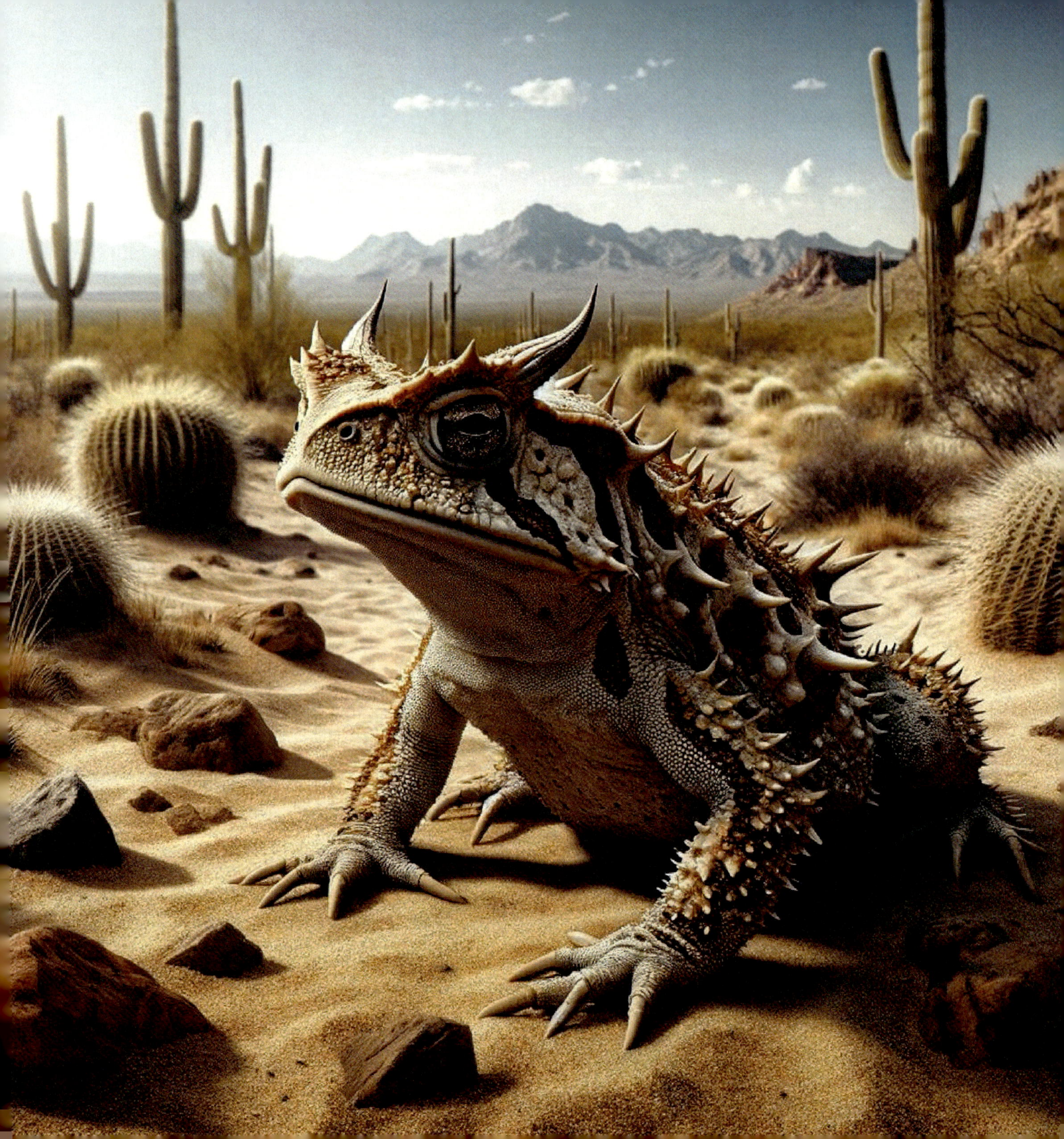

Horned Toad

The horned toad isn't actually a toad at all; it's a lizard with a really cool name! These little creatures are famous for their spiky appearance, including horns on their heads that make them look like tiny dinosaurs. They are mostly found in deserts and dry, sandy places, blending in perfectly with their surroundings thanks to their brown and sandy-colored skin. Horned toads are pretty small, usually about the size of a tea cup, making them hard to spot. They love to eat ants and other small insects, using their sticky tongues to catch their meals. Despite their fierce look, horned toads are harmless to humans and can be quite shy. When they feel scared or threatened, they might puff up their bodies to look bigger and more intimidating to predators. Horned toads are fascinating creatures that remind us of how amazing and varied nature can be!

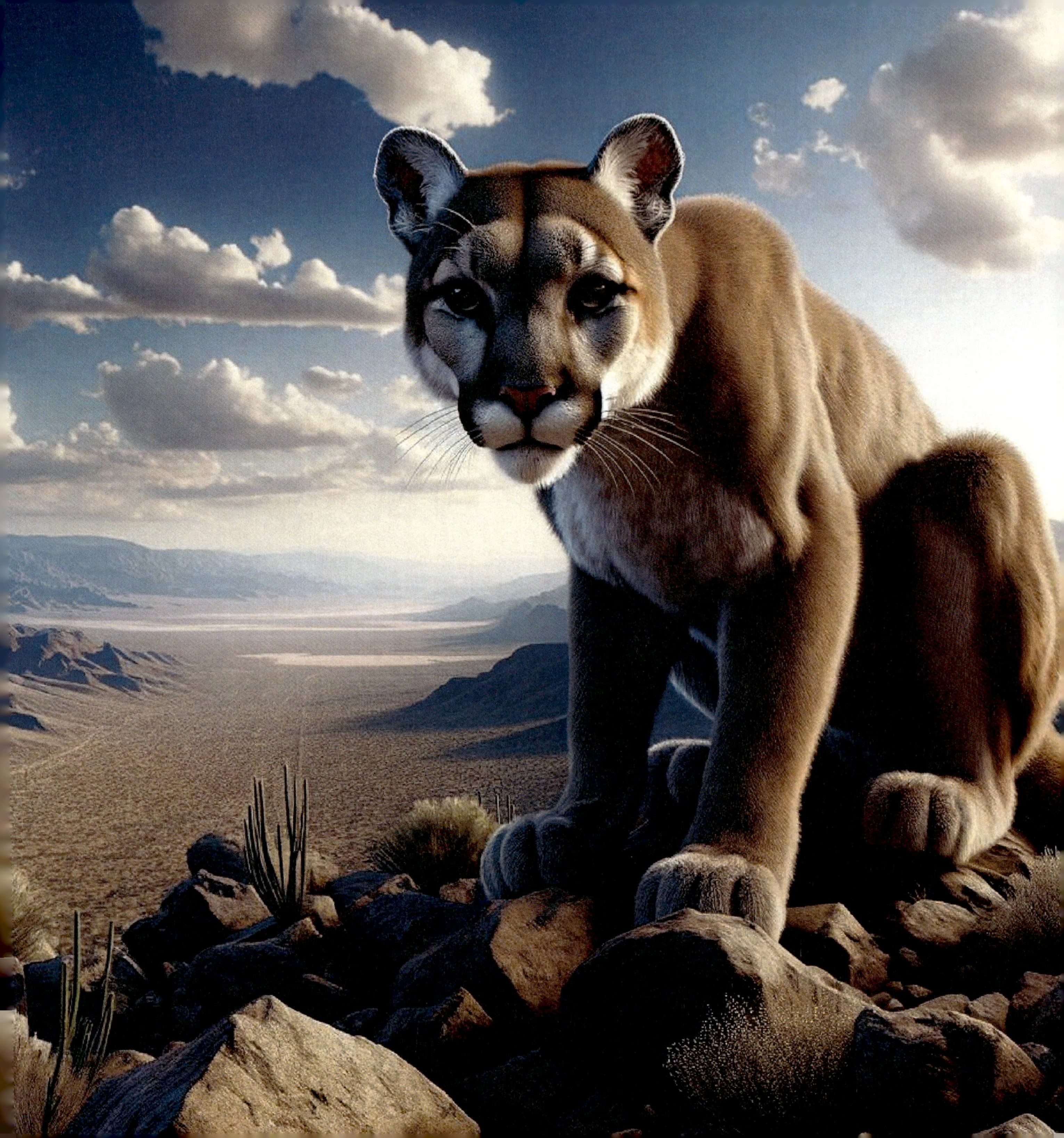

Mountain Lion

Mountain lions are big, wild cats that live in many places, including forests, mountains, and deserts. They are also known as cougars or pumas, and they have beautiful tan or light brown fur that helps them hide in their natural surroundings. Mountain lions are very strong and fast, which makes them excellent hunters. They prefer to live alone and are very territorial, which means they like to have their own space. Despite their fierce reputation, mountain lions are shy and usually avoid people. They are most active during dawn and dusk when they go out to find food, like deer and smaller animals. Mountain lions can jump really high and far, even up to 15 feet in the air and 40 feet forward in one leap! They play an important role in keeping the balance of nature by helping control the population of other animals. Remember, if you're ever exploring their home areas, it's important to respect their space and keep a safe distance.

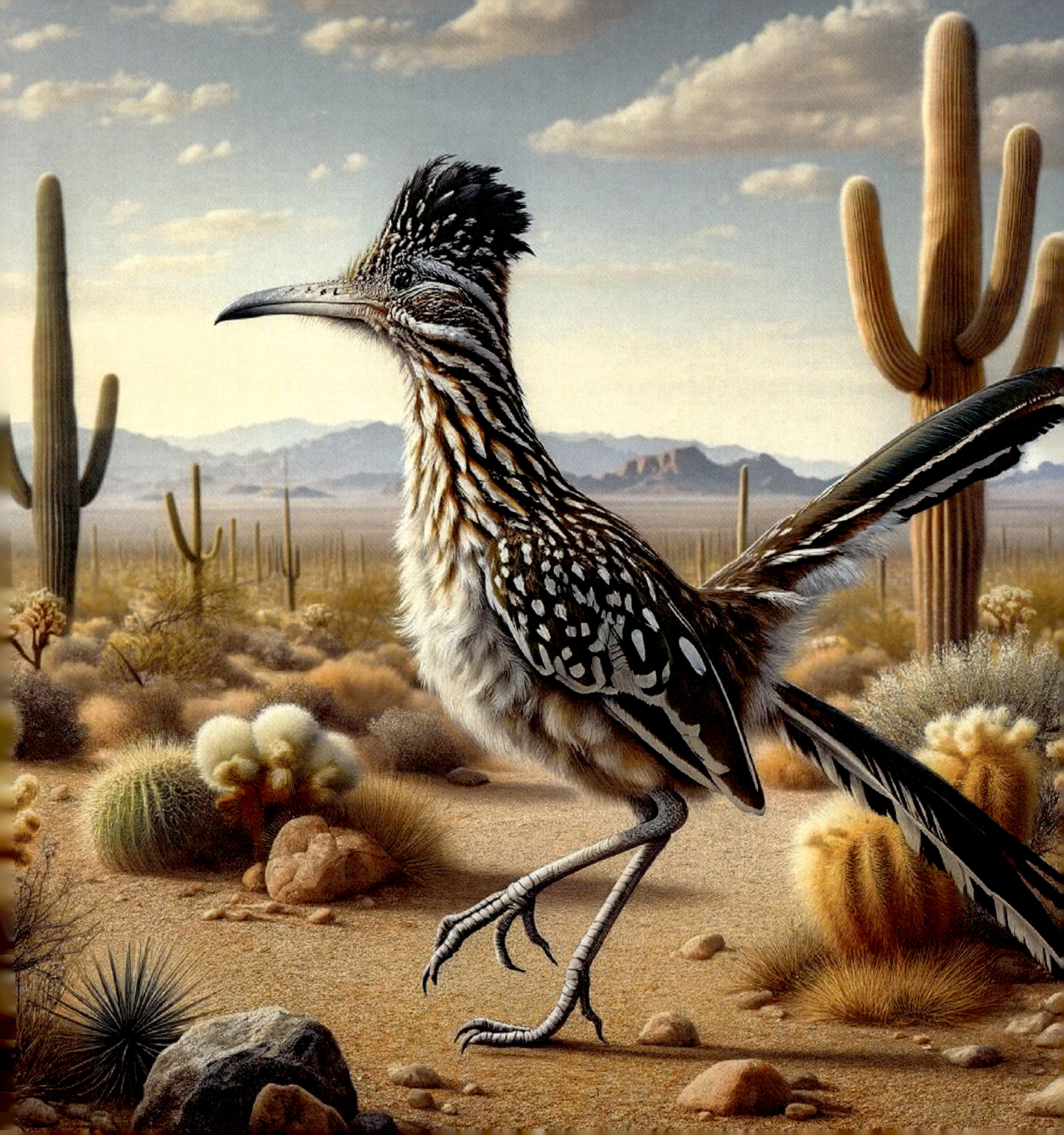

Roadrunner

Roadrunners are super cool birds that are more likely to run on the ground than fly. They have long legs, a long tail, and a crest on their head, which is a bunch of feathers that stands up. Their name comes from their habit of racing across roads in front of cars, reaching speeds of up to 20 miles per hour! That's faster than you can ride your bike! Roadrunners live in the deserts and scrublands of the southwestern United States and Mexico. They are amazing hunters and can eat lots of different things, like insects, lizards, and even small snakes. What's really fun about roadrunners is that they are very curious and aren't afraid to check out their surroundings, including people. They have a unique look with their green and blue feathers that shimmer in the sunlight. Roadrunners are not just fast; they are smart, too, making them one of the most interesting birds you might find in the desert.

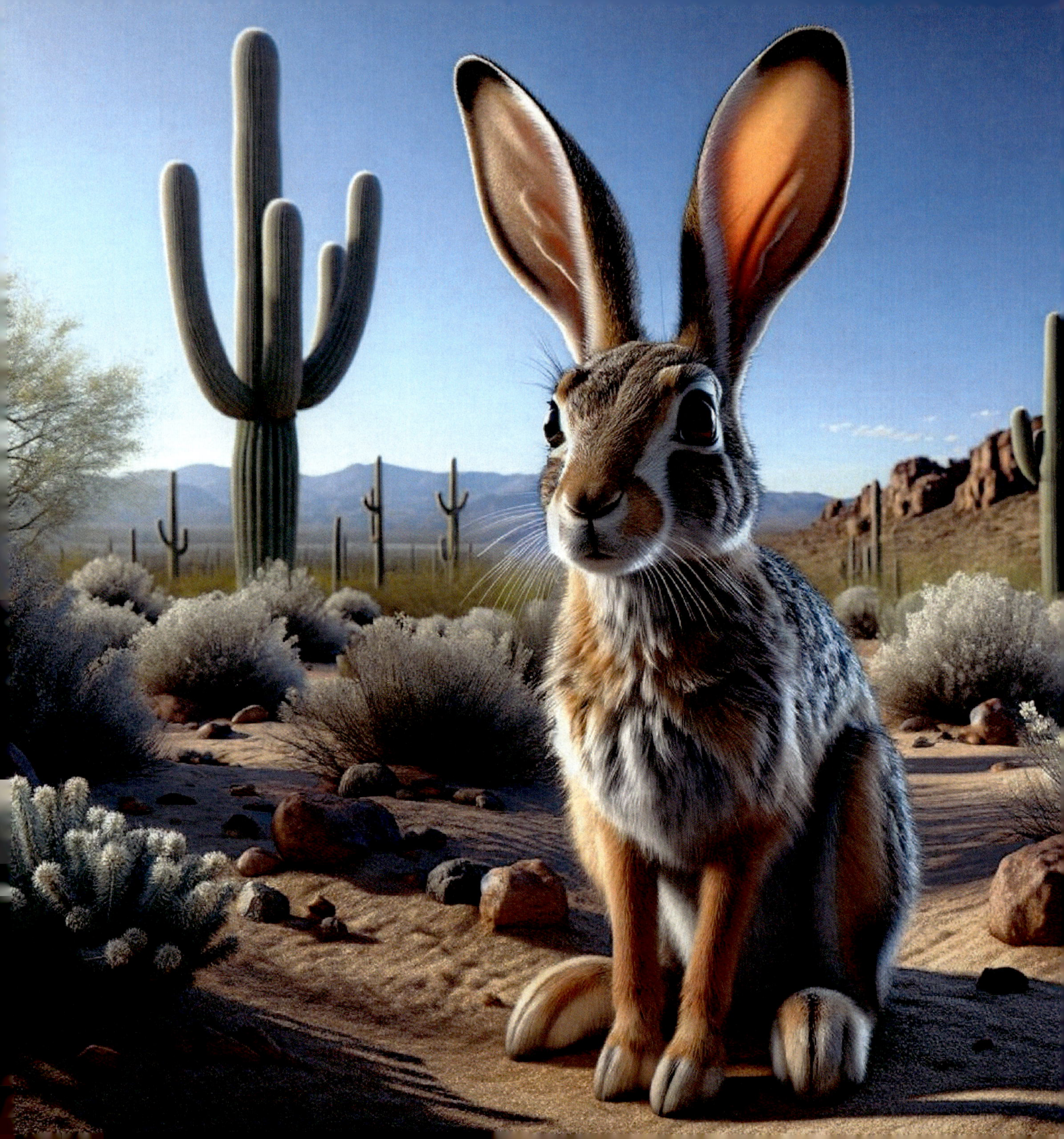

Jackrabbit

Jackrabbits are not actually rabbits, but they are really big hares that live in the deserts, plains, and forests. They have very long ears that can be as long as their head, and these ears help them stay cool in the hot sun. Their fur is usually a mix of brown, gray, and white, which helps them blend into their surroundings and hide from predators. Jackrabbits are known for their incredible speed; they can run up to 40 miles per hour and make big leaps of up to 10 feet in one jump when they're trying to escape danger. They are mostly active during the cool times of the day, like early morning and late evening. Jackrabbits eat plants, including grasses, herbs, and the bark of young trees. Their big eyes give them a wide field of vision, which is super helpful for spotting predators from far away. Jackrabbits are fascinating creatures that have some pretty cool ways to survive in the wild!

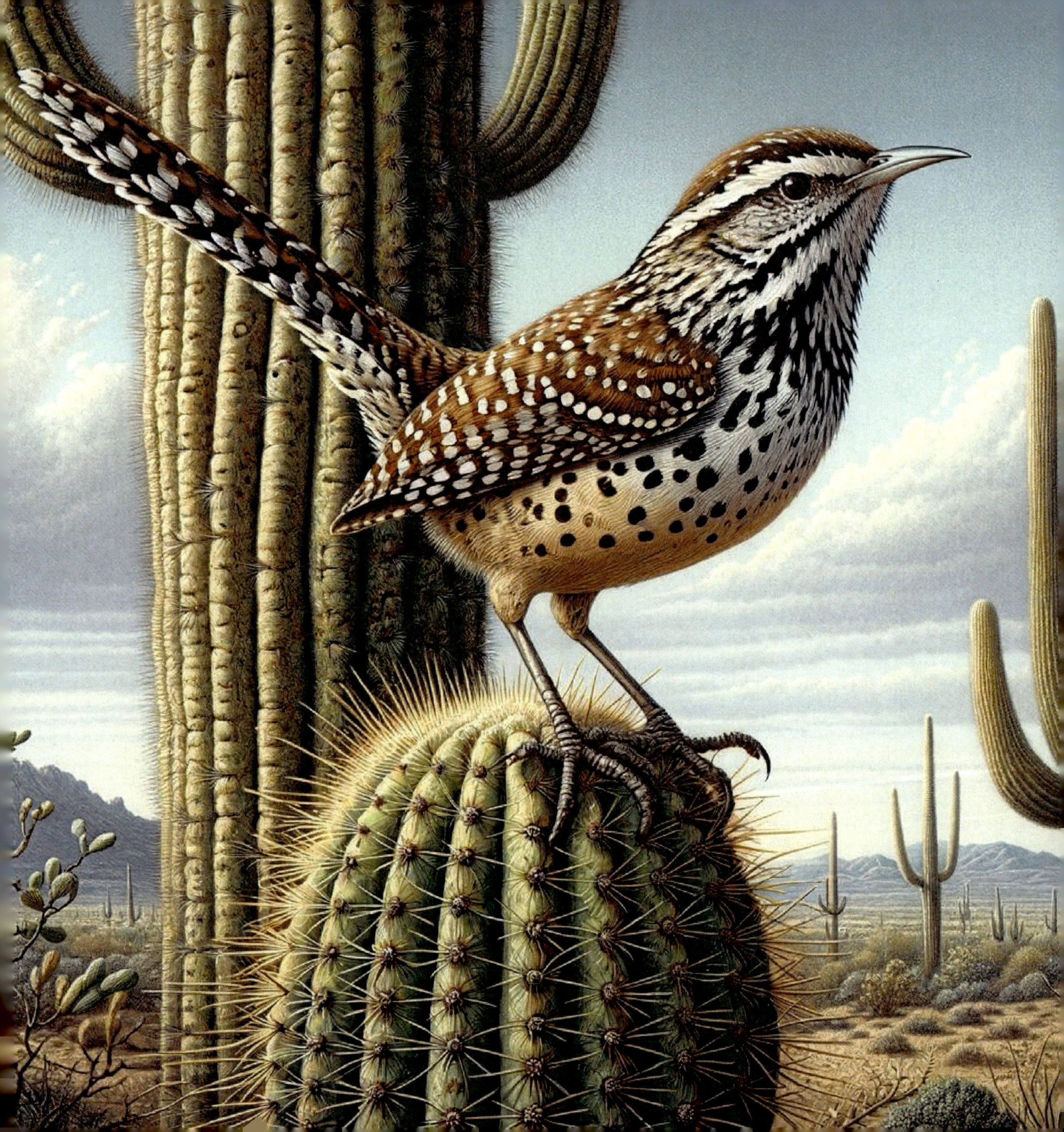

Cactus Wren

The cactus wren is a special bird that lives in the deserts of the southwestern United States, and it's also the state bird of Arizona. It has a brown and white streaky body, with a long tail and a stout beak, making it look quite unique and easy to recognize. Cactus wrens are amazing because they build their nests in cactus plants, using the sharp spines for protection against predators. These nests are not just any nests; they're shaped like a football and have a side entrance, which makes them really cool and safe homes for the wren's eggs and babies. Cactus wrens are very active during the day, hopping around in search of insects and spiders to eat. They have a loud and distinctive call that sounds like a car engine starting, which they use to talk to each other. These birds are not only fascinating to learn about but also show us how animals can adapt to live in challenging places like the desert.

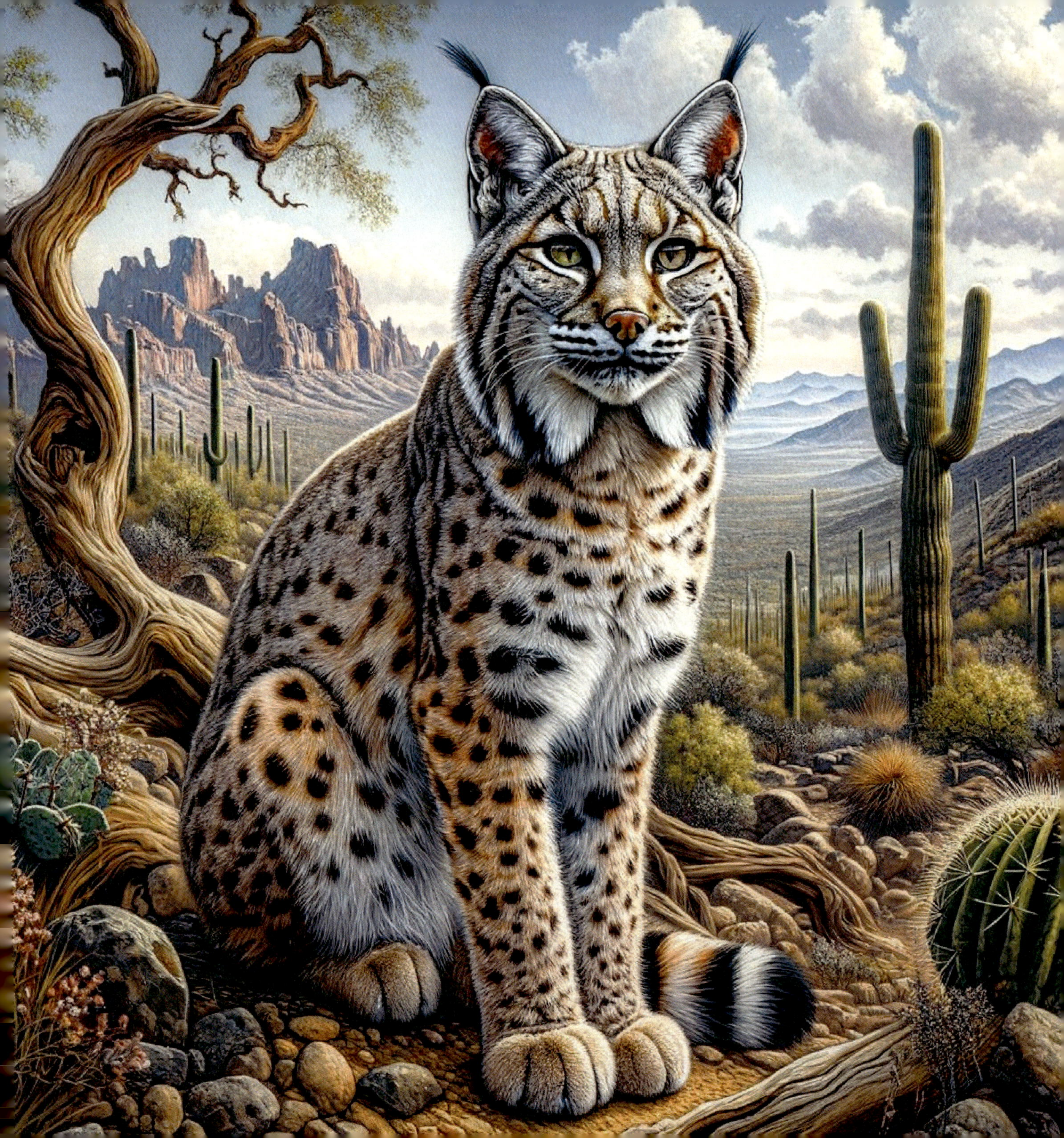

Bobcat

Bobcats are wild cats that live in forests, deserts, and even near where people live. They're called bobcats because of their short, or "bobbed," tails. These cats are medium-sized, with beautiful brown or reddish fur that has black spots and stripes, which helps them hide when they're hunting for food. Bobcats are very sneaky and quiet, making them excellent hunters. They eat small animals like rabbits, birds, and sometimes deer. Even though they're wild, bobcats are very shy and usually avoid humans. They are mostly active at night, but it's not unusual to see them during the day, especially at dawn or dusk. Bobcats are amazing climbers and swimmers, which means they can explore many different places. They're incredible animals that show us how adaptable and skilled nature can be!

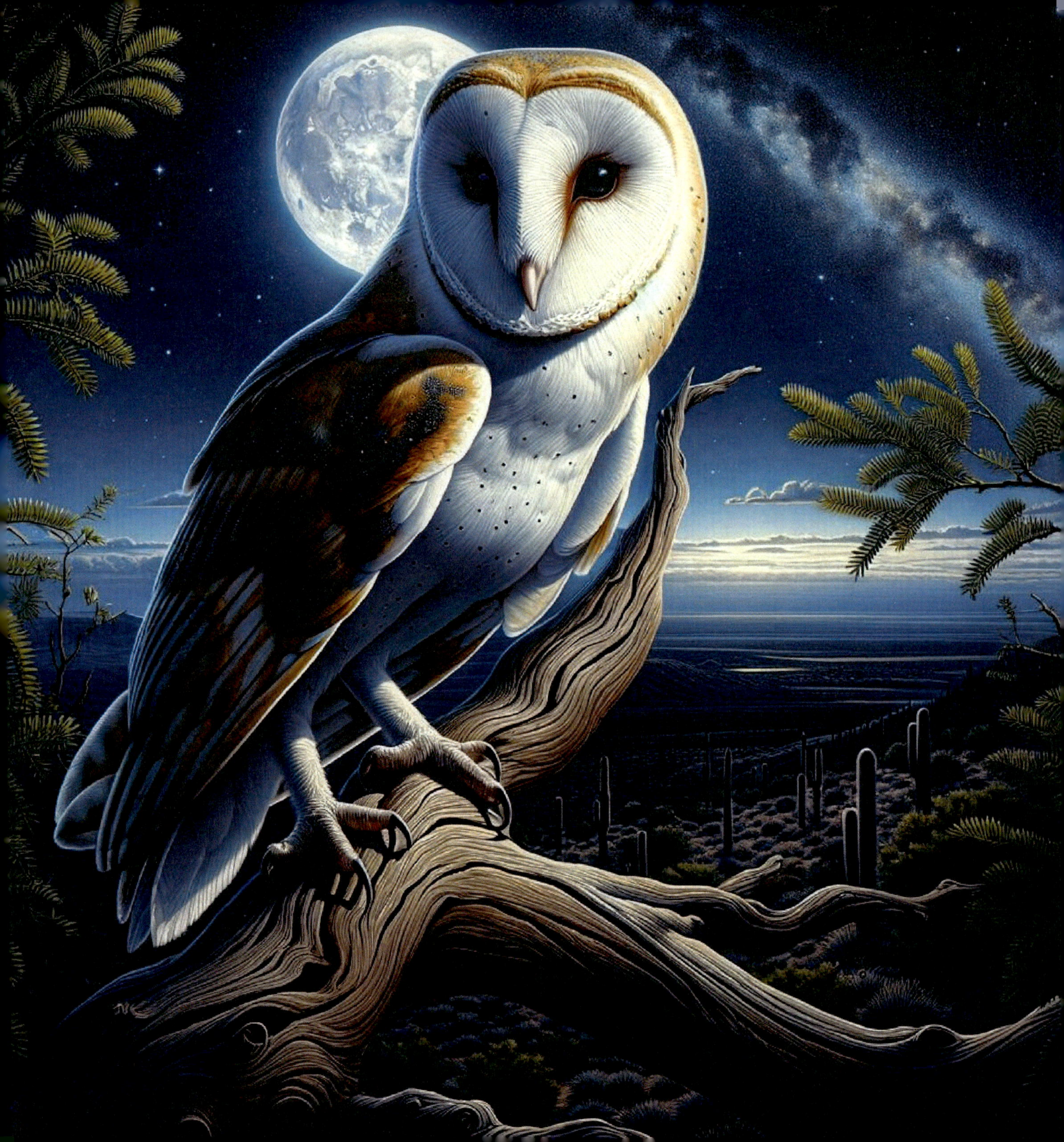

Barn Owl

Barn owls in Arizona are fascinating birds with a magical appearance. They have a heart-shaped face, big, round eyes, and a pale body that can almost seem to glow in the moonlight. These owls are not very big, but they have impressive wings that help them fly silently through the night. Barn owls are great at catching mice, rats, and other small animals because of their super sharp hearing. They can even hear a tiny creature moving beneath the grass or leaves! They like to live in quiet places, like the open deserts and fields of Arizona, and sometimes in barns or other old buildings, which is how they got their name. Barn owls make a screeching sound instead of the hooting we usually expect from owls. They are helpful to farmers because they eat lots of pests. Seeing a barn owl can be a special treat, as they are mysterious and beautiful creatures of the night.

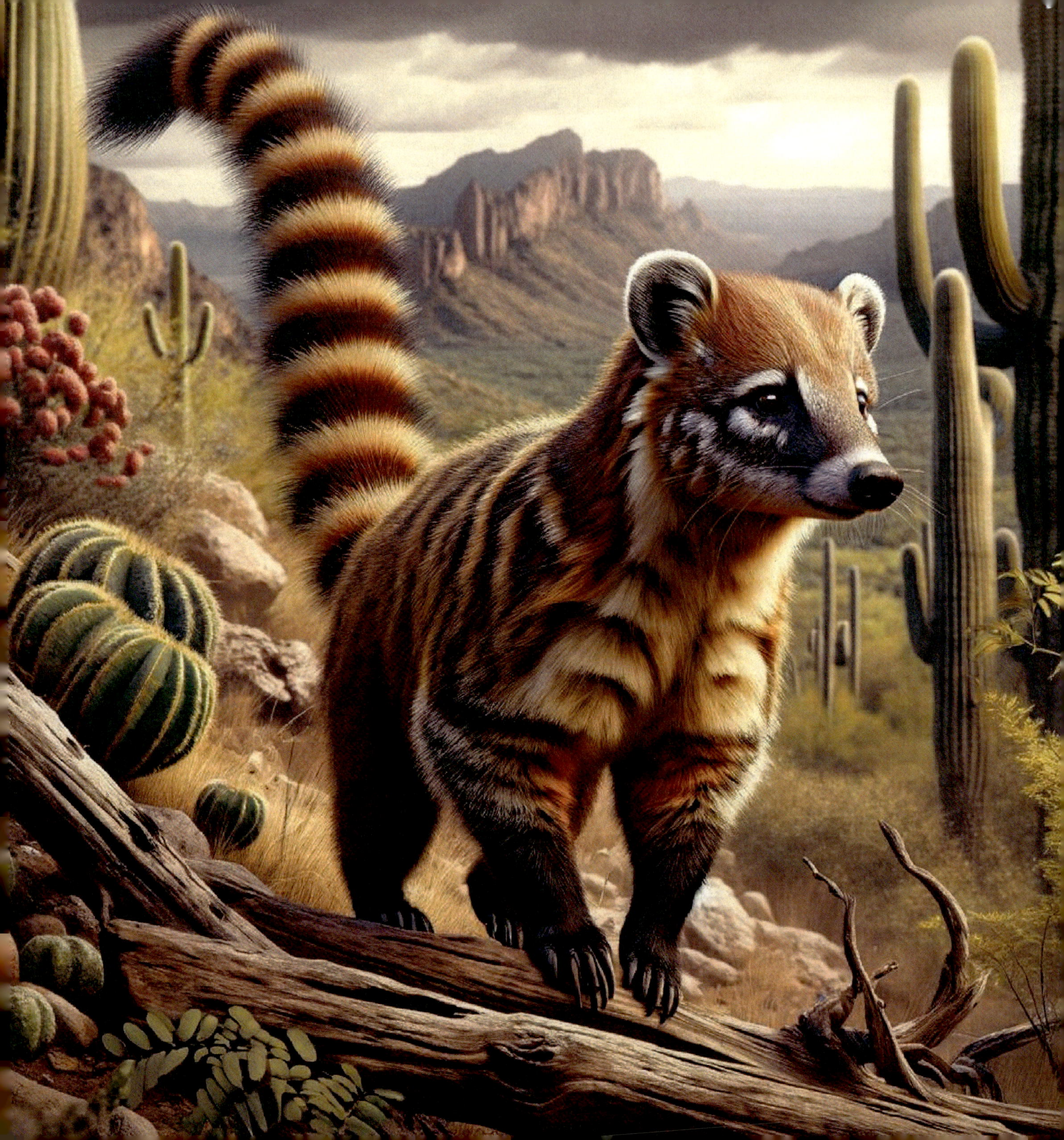

Coatimundis

Coatimundis, or "coatis," are curious and playful animals that look a bit like raccoons with their masked faces and bushy tails. They live in the forests and canyons of Arizona, where they roam around in groups called bands. Coatis have long noses that they wiggle around to sniff out their food, which can be fruits, insects, and small animals. They are excellent climbers and spend a lot of their time in trees, searching for tasty snacks or taking a nap in the branches. Coatis are known for their social nature, often seen playing or foraging for food together. They communicate with each other through a variety of sounds, from whistles to grunts. These animals are quite the adventurers and are always on the move, exploring their surroundings with curiosity and agility. Seeing a coatimundi in the wild can be an exciting experience, as they are unique and interesting creatures of the Arizona wilderness.

The End

Thanks for Reading

Made in United States
North Haven, CT
04 December 2024